THE SHAPES THAT SHELTER TAKES

poems by

Judith Kleck

Finishing Line Press
Georgetown, Kentucky

THE SHAPES THAT SHELTER TAKES

Copyright © 2025 by Judith Kleck
ISBN 979-8-89990-053-2 First Edition
All rights reserved under International and Pan-American Copyright Conventions. No part of this book may be reproduced in any manner whatsoever without written permission from the publisher, except in the case of brief quotations embodied in critical articles and reviews.

ACKNOWLEDGMENTS

A special thanks to the editors who published a number of these poems: *The Ellensburg Anthology, The Hawaii Review, Hubbub, The Montana Review, Panoply, Poetry Northwest, Pontoon #1-3, The Seattle Review, Southern Poetry Review, The Washington English Journal*. Four poems were included in the anthology *Deep Down Things: Poems of the Inland Pacific Northwest*. Thanks as well to Richard Denner who published her chapbook *Winter Fruit*, and to Finishing Line Press who published her other chapbook *Culling the Petals*.

This book was made possible in part by donations to the ONE LAST WORD Program. ONE LAST WORD helps to bring the last works of gifted poets to the world.

Publisher: Leah Huete de Maines
Editor: Christen Kincaid
Cover Art: Rob Fraser
Author Photo: Joseph Powell
Cover Design: Elizabeth Maines McCleavy

Order online: www.finishinglinepress.com
also available on amazon.com

Author inquiries and mail orders:
Finishing Line Press
PO Box 1626
Georgetown, Kentucky 40324
USA

Contents

Foreword 1

1. *Together & Alone*

   Portrait 4
   My Father Walks 5
   Quince 6
   Egg 7
   Listening to My Parents Make Love 8
   At Odds 9
   Pigeons 10
   Cargo 12
   Sonnets for Seasons & Friends 13
   Steam Heat 15
   Madera Canyon 16
   Pastoral 17
   Ellensburg Blues 18
   A Valentine 19
   On the Day Before You Returned 20
   Makers of Ceremony 21
   Peonies 23
   A Vile Cheer 24
   Dancing 25
   Widower: Sequim 27
   Amen, Boys 28
   Whidbey Island: Meditations 29

2. *Navigating Loss*

   Sleep 32
   Haiku at 6:00 A.M 33
   Impromptu 34
   Jester 35
   Frog Song 36
   The Waiting Air 37
   Hope for the Children of Poets 38
   Ridge Lines 40
   Red Hills and Bones 41
   Circumnavigating Loss 42
   Sunday at St. Andrew's 43
   Not Easy 44
   Flowers: Memorial Day 45
   Two Years 46
   Sober and Sane 47
   Speaking to the Dead 48

3. Sweeter Still

    Morning Songs 50
    Deconstructing Heart 51
    Gravity: Semantics 52
    Logic 53
    Drift 54
    Periodic Tableau 55
    You and I 56
    Limits 57
    What Waits to be Said? 58
    Green Valley, March 59
    Berry Picking 60
    The Day is Suddenly Longer 61
    Horses 62
    Epiphanies at Forty-Eight 63
    Crows 64
    Bread and Wine 65
    This Night 66
    Branding Time 67
    Winter Fruit 69

4. Olive Light

    In Olive Light 72
    Still Life: Zakynthos 73
    A Calling 74
    Athens & Anasazi 75
    In Kiffisia 76
    Meltemi 77
    The Greek Sun 78
    Homesick 79
    Arrival 80
    Wild Strawberries: Reecer Creek 81

5. Against Silence

    Li Ch'ing-chao in the CCU 84
    Chimayo 85
    Walking on Stilts 87
    I am thinking of my Grandmother's House on Steele Street ... 89
    Against Silence 90
    The Red-Winged Blackbirds are Back 91
    poem of one thumb 92
    Silence 93
    Toward Earth 94
    Last Boat Ride 95
    A Poem Considering Love 96
    This Body of Desire 97
    The Last Word 99

Afterword 101

Foreword

Judith Kleck wrote poetry rather reluctantly over the course of thirty-four years, until her death from A.L.S. in 2012, at the age of 62. From 1978-80 she did graduate work in poetry in the MFA program at the University of Arizona. Although she loved language and could be intensely interested in writing poems, other demands on her time always seemed to take precedence: teaching, being a mother, a wife, a friend, a gourmet cook.

Because we taught together in the same English department, she used her maiden name, Kleck, rather than confuse students with two Powells. She also used Judith Kleck as her writing name; however, she legally changed her name to Judith Kleck Powell after retiring. I wanted to honor her writing name because her previously published books and poems were under that name.

When she was diagnosed with A.L.S., she began writing a blog called *In Dog Years I'm Dead* which soon had 1,200 followers. She also wrote poems to include in that blog which are in the last section of this book. I've arranged the poems using both thematic and chronological threads, but a thematic placement always trumped chronological allegiance. For example, the abuse poems were written later, but are about that early part of her life, so I placed them in the first rather than the third section. She did not date her poems, but we began to write poems at nearly the same time (1976), so I'm relying primarily on memory for the chronological sequence.

Judy's interests were wide: teaching, breaking and training horses, flyfishing, cooking, writing, reading, knitting, mushrooming, agate hunting, playing music—piano, guitar, and harmonica. She had a marvelous ear for the sounds and textures of language, and her poems could be heart-breakingly honest. She loved language games like Scrabble and Bookworm, creating anagrams and finding words inside any sequence of letters. Some of that wordplay is evident in poems like "Deconstructing Heart" and "You and I." She was essentially a lyric poet who examined issues of aging, gender, abuse, relationships, travel, and the effects of her disease, all with an unflinching clarity and emotional exactness.

She published two chapbooks, *Culling the Petals*, from Finishing Line Press, and *Winter Fruit* from dPress, but she rarely sent poems out for publication. I discovered a few poems on her computer and in a notebook after she died. This project of collecting and arranging her poems was a way to both honor her memory and appreciate that inner life of poetry which throughout her career was mostly private.

Her favorite poets were Emily Dickinson, Theodore Roethke, Li Ch'ing-Chao (three imitations of her style are included here), William Stafford, and Linda Pastan. Music, emotional resonance, an earthy centeredness, and precision were the guiding principles for her appreciation of poetry, the construction of her own poems, and living her life. —Joseph Powell

TOGETHER & ALONE

PORTRAIT

I am nervous, I say,
to sit this way, so still
so long, to be the one described
by the eye, the hand, of another
who looks hard at the world.
I'm afraid to see what she
won't in me. I have no look,
and worse, I want to laugh
to break the mood like glass—
let the pieces be enough.

The good ones come fast,
she says, but the day draws on
and I sit for three. I'm not the muse
I'd hoped to be, but a strong face,
every feature sure as this gray day
dulling the window, sure as the rain
I'll walk out into.

MY FATHER WALKS

across an open field, head down.
Alfalfa blooms, yearlings fatten in the sun.
He is a tender of cattle, a tender of grasses,
wheat and hay. His hands are large
and gnarled. Now they swing softly
at his sides, silent bells, blunted scythes,
that stroke the purple heads, brush them lightly,
as if he feels sorry for the price he will ask,
the price they will pay.

He pulls a knot of blossoms,
holds them like a bouquet.
Then he looks up,
sees me watching and waves.

For a moment I think he is going to…

then he crushes them between his palms,
and tosses them, casually, away.

QUINCE

Pausing under a tree
my mother muddles pluralities:
quince or *quinces*?
talking through heat and summer
with its scent of readiness
and fruit. We filled our blouses
and sunk in orchard grass,
it could have been Africa
we held in our arms,
a continent never crossed.

We split the fruit, scooped
the seeds, and I wanted to be
in her woman's body,
to feel myself unfold
flesh into flesh.
But I thought words
would fail us then,

so I loved the summer
for its obvious greed and pinned
Napoleon above my bed—
not for the man but the horse,
coiled and carved like a tree.

Late in summer, beneath the elms,
false love/first sex. I wanted
to think of exotic lands
but shadows were light
I could not see until this morning

when light lifted the grass
and horses lipped plums half seriously,
the word came back, a taste forgotten—
quince. Her hands thickening
the fruit with honey, our elbows
touching over the sink
trusting at last that common silence
from which we'll begin again.

EGG

After books, watching for mother,
I found the shells,
blue and broken and, sometimes,
the fallen chicks, mostly dead,
but one or two with slight life left,
I carried home. In my hand
their weight was not the egg's.
They always died, but

in my books the horses
kicked ass and did their noble deeds.
Their lives had weight and meaning:
one saved the herd from fire,
another from a man.

What is it that leads us back
to small significance? To the sensuous
drift of a wither down the fall
line to the chest? What plays
clearer than the single note
of the egg, heavy against
the palm's treble clef?

But now, the weight of an egg
in the palm is enough
to slow me down,
the perfect curl of shell,
its brown & brittle containment,
a small fact that anyone might know.

LISTENING TO MY PARENTS MAKE LOVE
    —*Taos, New Mexico, La Hacienda de Blanco*

It is being at the intersection of two moments—
there, when Julio Mateo slams the perfect
pitch, outside corner low and away and Jeter
swings and misses, 3 & 2, even though New York
goes on to win, that pitch, that moment holds.

Like the night I lay awake and listened to my parents
make love three feet to the left, heard the notes my mother
muffled to keep from giving it away,
the sad grunt of my father saying it ended too soon.

This is the intersection of beauty and its opposite.
The pitch streams across the plate,
catching the outside corner
maybe one quarter inch, but catching as the breath
catches at the moment of climax, the perfect pitch of
Oh against the blankness of No. This is the moment
when all's sacrificed to what's to become.

It is the difference a fraction makes: one quarter
of forever begs to differ, be it an inch, an hour,
a life poorly lived. And my mother,
humbled by orgasm, my father emblazoned,
and me wondering what, if anything, could be
true, could be truer than catching the outside
corner in the dark and against such odds.

AT ODDS

That's what we were.
Both born in the ninth month
in even years: forty-eight
and fifty. This year, those
also mark our ages. Therefore,
brother, I propose a toast:

Here's to your knees,
scuffed that night you crawled
into my room. Only saints
deserve such pilgrimage.

Here's to your hand,
the one that found my budding
breast. Swarm of bees
on a bird's nest.

Here's to the other hand
that made its way between
my thighs. Dull saw seized
in green wood.

Here's to the dog
whose name I called
instead of yours: to say
yours made it real.

So, let me say it now,
for you were there in that room
with me, Jack.

Those were your hands
in my bed. I've held them
long enough. Take them back

as just this year
I took my body back.
Let's call it even at last.

We'll toast the girl
who's outlasted shame,
the boy who could own
the blame he could never imagine.

We've come full circle
to start again, hands outstretched
feeling our way through the dark.

PIGEONS

They were my brother's miracle,
bred to fly unknown miles
back to the stone coop
in a canyon where the Gallico creek
took a last hard turn
before disappearing south.
Each new house meant a new flock,
squabs to fledge and feed.
Was it the surety of home he needed,
the right range to fly, or proof
that something was his own
and would return to him alone?
A young boy's romance of flight
riveted to the stars?

I lost my brother to his adolescent greed
the night his hands found my breasts,
my crotch, the constellation of his wonder.
So began the pure distrust: me of him,
he of himself. We spoke across
a distance charted by blame,
our worlds circling, cautious
as pigeons searching for a roost.

Now our lives are mostly lived,
children with children of their own,
the aches of aging settle in.
Our homes fold down around us
like tired flesh on bone.
The birds are long gone,
the coop a rockery of crumbling stone.
How should we find our way
back? What stars can give direction?

What little trust we have left
will never be enough but it is
ours, together and alone.
Love needs such a compass
to pull us through the shame,
an instinct pinned to a single
point of light, unnamed.

But once we loved each other.
Once we called the same place home,
shared a name. Once believed
in the miracle of a bird
breaching the horizon.

One imagined pigeon still circles
in the thinning air.

CARGO

In my mother's dream
the plane that's going down
is huge and slow, a cargo ship
weighted with the goods of her life.
But she is not on that plane
and so is implicated in its failing.

In my dream the plane is full of tourists
descending into tropical seas. It is burning
and beautiful and arcs nose up
into the night, holds, a cross ignited
before it drops. I am not on that plane
but implicated in the drama of its falling.

My mother has grown smaller now.
When I hold her, she is lost in my arms.
Her face translucent and soft,
her eyes still blue and shy
and I don't want to lose her.

When I was five, she held me
close and told me what she'd dreamed.
Held me fast against her doubts,
afraid of losing me. I see now

we were both beautiful then
and burning, falling toward water.

SONNETS FOR SEASONS & FRIENDS

January 1969: India

Geology was our excuse to drink:
that class depressed us, rocks gray with names
mythology would love. We needed blame
to fall beyond us, something cold to think

past Vietnam, those friends already sinking
in its wake. How much of us was claimed
by bitterness? By loss? The winter came
as no surprise that year; the snow was zinc

white and deep. We drifted with it. Lost
into deliberate lives and men, we learned
to hide. And now the shock of ice along

the Spit recalls that winter night we almost
believed our luck would change. But cold still burns,
snow pelts the beach, & all seems strangely wrong.

March 1989: Marn

The storm held back another day. Along
the beach the peeps and plovers fed and preened.
I walked and watched 'til watching seemed a screen,
a blind within the brightening drift of spring.

A killdeer frets the water; gulls belong
to one another now, and so they scream
with fresh intention, feeding still on need,
affection's hungry mate. The old squaw's song

is tireless on the bay; I thought of you
again today and wondered at the bond
that heedless in its caring, carries on.

The loons are changing plumage, though a few,
uncertain in the course the season's found,
find habit's heart still claiming most what's gone.

June: Lianne

Here spring's a constant. Daffodils persist
for weeks and green, like heat, oppresses. Rain
again. Three days now it's played that same
toccata. Lonely for the season's shift,

some variance of light or tone, I listen
to Vivaldi's Four. So much is changed
by repetition: music, faces, names,
those summer hills we hiked. Though we resist,

each change requires its loss. When overcast
some days I think I even miss the dust.
But memory lives on borrowed colors. What

we need most to believe about the past
will turn in season, bright or dark, adjust
itself to shade, to light, as bloom, as root.

September: Bobbie

Across the Juan de Fuca Strait, northeast
and out of nothing, Baker stuns the thin
blue air. How odd the mountain first should bring
the art to mind: impossible to see

it free of Hokusai, or you, your lean
collages, strong and spare, where color swings
its object open like a door. I think
of loves we share—shades of green, Matisse,

the rituals of food. Yet separate arts
define our separate lives. A heron keels
across the sound. We are absorbed by these

inventions, puzzling mountains into parts
until a suddenness of vision yields
a wholeness up: relinquished, we are blessed.

STEAM HEAT

The stage has a darkness
the corners of coals
and deepest off-center
where jazz-lady holds
herself to the music
then hip curl up
through the light
like smoke
knee-nudging-shoulder-shimmy
everybody's still
just watching miz jazz bones
making it real
killing it slow
& down to the floor
carving her S's
out of thigh and toes

essess, we got steam heat,
sst, sst, steam heat.

MADERA CANYON

Under scrub oak and piñon pine
you spread a coat, unpack bread
and cheese, wine, a cheap red,
French, bottled the year I left
a husband and son. I raise it
to their good fortune, to all
forgotten feasts. Eight years

of marriage, of looking out windows
past barbed wire fences
bowed as the backs of old horses,
past the weedy and whittled edges
of the farm, the run-down dairy
we tried to call home. Even the trees,

seemed weary. Slate gray, wind-worn,
they managed to bloom: Jonathans,
Bartletts, Elbertas, Romes. I simmered
with them in kitchen pots, took their names
for comfort, refused my own.

After dinner, we didn't talk
and pushing a chair from the table
was not a simple act, or thoughtless,
but the distance our lives divided
into, even as these grapes were lugged
to vats, even as this cheese quickened
in its skin on a foreign shelf.

Old world. Old wounds. We belong
to what we choose to remember; the rest
will find us, in time. But here, the wine
breathes, cheese sweats, you speak to me
in human terms, familiar sounds—
each syllable a risk you shape
deliberately towards change.

PASTORAL

Look up and out: the window opens
on a scene too pastoral. This house
surrounded by fields, alfalfa and clover,
peopled by cows whose mottled
and matronly bodies keep our country time—
morning to milk, evening to feed,
what else happens, happens simply,
in between.

What impossible romance holds me here
to words, and how? What tongue-in-cheek,
what tug & pull at speech's sleeve
wants to call an owl an *arabesque of sound?*
A cow a *stutter in the green?*

As words wear thin, enchantment
shows its bitter end, and who wants more
some soft & pretty syllable to hide within?

And yet, patient as those cows who,
dark and graceless, now come back
to feed, I wait for the final say:
honesty's thief in the broad light of day.

ELLENSBURG BLUES
for Joe

I refuse to count days
hearing a marriage that lasts
seven years would last forever.

Now beneath the bridge
I used to cross, wanting a way
out or in again, we've stopped
to turn stones searching for agates
this valley and Tibet provide. We
refuse to undo this puzzle, roughly
exotic, return each rock
to its familiar place.

Blue one, blue one. My words weave
like grasses leaning with the river.

Evening we mark time by pages
turned and I imagine we read
the same words, in different orders,
taking separate languages
to a common bed. Your reticence
undone by the body's stark commitment,
your shoulders knotted as the rock
I turned in my hands.

Blue one, blue one. Your love's a stone
I take, I give back again.

A VALENTINE

I left without saying anything
so my silence might become the words
you wouldn't pause to hear.
I thought you didn't notice. That night
I ignored your questions and requests.
The silence could have honed a knife.

We became the shadows we walked through.
I edged to my side of the bed,
you stared at the ceiling.
Finally, sleepless, we had it out—
accusations, tears, resolutions.
The next day, poppies and irises,
a fine wine and chocolates.

For twenty years, our few impasses have passed
without a shame the world would have a name for,
without a word that didn't have the strength to die.
Within contention is a dream:
the petalfall foretells another flower.
We are kept alive by all our striving:
a poppy shines more brilliantly for falling.

ON THE DAY BEFORE YOU RETURNED

a flock of sparrows startled
the tree beyond my bedroom door.
I was alone.

I thought of your hands,
heavy over a cup of tea,
steam sifting, then lost,
a rush of wings denying shape.

So memory fails as love fails,
at the heart of things most common.
And your voice. Will it fly too
with the sparrow?

after Li Ch'in-chao

MAKERS OF CEREMONY

I

Gauguin could not contain his women,
their arms grown to the thickness of thighs,

grown into volumes of flesh, phosphorescent
and linear as evening in Tahiti, as this hour

now pressing into the bulk of night, where you,
given up to this room, lie naked on a sheet,

keeping watch over the dead watching, over the violets
on the sill, bluer this time and violently social.

His women crossed their ankles and died,
or spread heavy legs against black canvas

to allow reversals of light, to make ritual
of the body's soft angles, of the angry colors

brown & green & red. Angry women,
makers of ceremony, mothers of every dying.

II

But what did he know of your own sweet loss,
of the child who lives, still, by the stroke
of your grief? Only that colors may speak:
Don't be afraid. Paint it as blue as you can.
Civilization is what makes you sick.

So against the blankness of desert heat
you've planted flowers. Dwarf zinnias,
nasturtiums, asters—a patch of fatal color.

III

I want soft hues to comfort you.
This morning in a letter I write
anger first, acceptance last,
but words couldn't find you.
So I walked the beach.

Above, through pine brake
the cow bells rolled their solitary note
down cliff-side trails. I listened for their song,

found a tide-thinned bone
and wanted it complete—
strung with shells, good luck
to wear between your breasts
and charm the body into belief.

But what we finally deny the unborn child,
the rites of birth, the rites of death,
we first deny ourselves and so our acts
become symbolic, drift without us

into clearer lives. Those Tillamook Jerseys,
slow and wet, move milk-heavy
toward an unseen barn, falling
one by one into darkness. What warmth,
what need, what dim note calls them there?

PEONIES

The peonies droop in early heat.
By noon, their petals heap the ground.
Red mountains

I would like to walk
in your woods. There I would find
the last of the early mushrooms—
cauliflower and morel.

I could fill
my skirt, dry them on strings above
the cold stove. In a late summer wind
they would make rasping music.

I am losing my voice
to hear yours. You have been gone
too long and already the peonies
are leaving.

after Li Ch'ing-chao

A VILE CHEER

Four boys in a red car,
out of school
in the sun & green heat
of spring. I think they

really meant no harm,
though what I saw in them,
even at a distance, was a shining
darkness, moonlight on metal.

I held my breath. Slowly
it passed, red & low to the ground,
then, "PIG!" It might have been *cunt*
or *spic* or *nigger* or *queer*—
that rasping growl,
that vile cheer.

I swerved in the bright light of May,
sure my neighbor—a quiet man who'd
spent the morning chopping wood,
sure he must have heard. I didn't turn,
I was that afraid of pity.

Inside again, I washed my hair,
changed my clothes and looked
at last into the mirror. It came to me
then—what I should have yelled
or thrown or gestured back.

Days later, hiking with a friend
and hidden, I cried and felt a sadness for us all
who use the world to our own abuse,
who rename it to destroy what little trust
we've come to share. Those small and careless

daily hurts undo us in the end.
Those boys were children still
out for fun in fine weather
but I find no comfort there

or here. Their shadows stalk me still
and seal a cool and deepening fear.

DANCING

> *Children dance before they hear the music.*
> —William Stafford

When I was five
I danced for the camera's
bright bar light, white curls
and a blue poodle skirt
spiraling, spinning,
so it would fly straight out
and encircle me like a plate.
I imagined myself a pretty
piece of cake. I imagined

I was the ballerina
who danced in my jewelry box:
lift the lid and she'd pop
ten hut and spin and spin
to the Blue Danube waltz.
A petit four in perfect form
icing the silvered glass.

But later, watching home movies,
she wasn't what I saw. The poodle skirt
and saddle shoes, yellow curls,
all were true, but the girl's body
was awkward and lewd.
Hands on hips, I Jack Lalaned.
Pelvic thrust, turn, thrust again.
In & out, forward back.
Where had I learned to dance like that?

*

My friend Ali did a Reno stint,
pony dancing above the heads
of tourists, gamblers, geeks.
Said the best girls made it to the stage;
fifteen years of ballet just to earn tassels
and the right to dance bare breasted in a cage.
She's thirty-four and she's not dancing anymore.

*

Evan is six. It's summer, mid-sandwiches
and pop, when the rain starts, drops
like sand through a sieve. He puts his food

back on his plate, stops, stands, begins to strip.
He's out the door and dancing, naked in the rain.

Arms outspread, he's spinning, spinning
head back, face up, tip-toed turning,
shivering, giggling, jiggling, a perfect eight.
Thunder booms—I should call him in.

Instead, I strip and run to dance
before the rain is gone, to dance
naked without music with my
dancing, laughing son.

WIDOWER: SEQUIM

Somewhere it ended, as always
and without ceremony.
Summer, the lust bound season,
spent in its own heat.

Where was I when it slipped by
like the death of a friend of a friend,
like all the deaths I read of here,
daily & anonymous.

Up from the tangle of shrubs,
juncos in cocky black flyer's caps
now scatter the seeds
and bother the rosy finches
into retreat.

The day advances full of birds,
their tireless comings & goings.
Next door the widower's woodpile
blocks his view of the bay.
He's lit an early fire;
smoke shifts into trees beyond—

and words no longer belong,
like summer or birds,
to what they once defined.
Yet the images linger,
the mourning they rely on.
The first cold wind is down
from the mountains where the season
has long since turned, pushing
the deer before it, forcing a winter song:

Names, be with us.
Wind, grieve gently over our heads.

AMEN, BOYS

Well, I was walking along like no big deal, like I shopped
Krydell's all the time. But I felt that purple bag smoothing
my thigh and heard that tissue paper whispering chic, chic, chick,
all the way. So I was in a pretty mind when I saw those boys
perched, loaded for game. I knew they'd seen me coming
and were laying plans, too. I slipped my bag to the other arm
see, so Krydell's would be eye high when I passed and they'd
think I had money and pull and might keep shut up quiet.

Next thing I know it's *Hey baby, sooey, sooey!* and I felt like somebody's
private parade. My mind shut down, but I kept working it, cause
I knew I'd have occasion to tell this story someday, though this
was headed to no good end. Suddenly some smoldering Mae West
miracle of a voice caught and turned me round to say, "*Hey boys,
know what I've got in this bag? One nasty little red silk peignoir. I bet
you don't even know what a PAINWHAR is, yeah? Well, why don't you just
look it up. Peignoir, boys, understand? Like I said, you should look it up.*"

Well, they didn't have time or mind to say much. They started
talking low and soft and I saw my work mobbing their lips, knew
they were working hard to say something big. But mostly, they were
praying they could hold onto that sweet piece of a word I'd tossed
them long enough to look it up: and I just kept on walking thinking
Amen, boys, amen.

WHIDBEY: MEDITATIONS

Thumb-drunk Bartok
plays in the swelling shade.
Vertigo consumes lacewing and gnat
and all day I have been thinking
of the light on Whidbey Island.

    *

Still in the sink,
last night's dishes and a bit
of bone from the lamb
seasoned with garlic and rosemary.
Spices linger in the curtains
like memory or the migraine's aura.

    *

The weather's intemperate.
Mountains rise like the backs
of whales, and from this distance
I imagine barnacles and the rough
smell of the ocean's edge.

    *

Tide flats. Crab husk. Blue heron
in a bluer haze.

    *

The tide wakens the blood,
draws the gull's eye to the snail.
The moon quickens in its shell.

NAVIGATING LOSS

SLEEP

creeps on like evening
colors, dull and weary
from heat. What anchors

me to the weight of day,
those papers to read,
those bills to pay?

Better to drift, to rock,
in the wake of image
as dream sets sail.

My eyes close.
The moment holds me
somewhere else
and nowhere.

Floating, sinking,
a boat going down
in heavy seas.

HAIKU AT 6:00 A.M.

Last night's snow was slight.
This morning the light won't wait
for the sun to rise.

Sleeping between two
male bodies, father & son,
I come up for air.

The old dog stretches
downward, turns three times around,
finds her shadow warm.

IMPROMPTU
> *for Sarn*

All morning at the piano
I think of nothing but
the uncontrollable notes
breaking out of reach.

Outside my neighbor whistles,
improvising a garden
beyond the steps
near the backyard fence

where last summer's scraps
of leaves and vines remind me
that Beethoven's *Adieu*
pays homage to such things.

I have grown a garden
with awkward hands,
thinned cabbages, tossed lettuce
to the garbage bin and felt in each
the weight of loss, the slightest sound.

Between each measure
I remember my son,
that each note has its own distinction,
how music becomes music
when nothing is played:

then I move as pure, transparent form,
abstract as the thumb's mute motion
towards the hand's correctness.

JESTER

Evan touches
where the jester hides
in him, just behind the breastbone,
close to the heart, caged by ribs.
He says, "Sometimes he's crazy.
Sometimes he just has to get out."

In class the clown is summoned
by questions my son can't answer,
a cute genie whose immature magic
makes the teacher scowl
and classmates titter.

At home he is messenger
of affections too large to contain
in this nine year old frame
whose child has yet
to turn against himself.

And so, I beseech you
little fool, big buffoon,
come out. Turn your cartwheels,
sing, juggle, dance and fart.

Make us laugh at your expense
and guard this boy's untutored heart.

FROG SONG

Among the cattails and willows
at the edge of the pond, their dank
repository of song, the frogs are making
music at the moon hidden beneath
a scum of cloud. Their notes
are ambitious; it's early spring,
the nights still cold enough
to demand attention.

Why should we listen
who spend our lives inside?
Why walk out under a veiled
light, to note our own silence
against this rough-cut sound,
seeking solace in such measures?

Still, I step out. At the creak
of my weight on the deck,
the frog song stops. We
learn each other's presence
in this absence of sound. We
wait it out: ten seconds, twenty

until one brave bull trumpets,
once, twice, and then two
and more until the night is full
again of their muscled music
large enough to make me small,
cold enough to tighten my nipples
against the wind.

Bark and bugle, burp and bellow,
banter boast bemoan their slick
slippery song of spawning stick
and ooze of mounting frenzied
fucking frogs among the suck
of mud and frond and mucoused moss:
we must, we must, we must.

I turn—obligingly, they stop
until the door clicks shut.
And I forget the words
for the poem I had thought
to write, the one about love
and silence and frog song
late and long into the night.

THE WAITING AIR
    for Sarn

What I've held like a clutch
all these years since you left

with your father was the fear
of letting you go knowing

you would come back changed
and find me strange as well:

my look, my clothes, my hair.
Knowing the intimate motions

we made through the day
would be heavier, more thoughtful

than before. So the simple hand
to the air could not be simple or careless

again. Still I raise my hand
to see you off, to feel the wind

and bring you back again to that day
in the park where we saw the pinwheel

pod of elm spin down and you asked
Do we have to die in heaven, too?

I said no as if I knew
and, like a shawl against some chill,

dropped my arm around you.
You shook my hug

and ran to swing, almost to the sky
and down again. *Push me, momma,*

higher, higher, farther, please.
I wave and laugh, push and sing.

You shout and lean against my hands,
the wind, my words,

working, shaping, changing the waiting air.

HOPE FOR THE CHILDREN OF POETS

When Lucinda sings
I step down the stairs
of those strings
and sit at the bottom
just to listen.

There's dust in her voice:
Southern and red
and relentless,
it holds its note
like a Texas horizon
holds sunup—
just long enough
to make you want more.
Just long enough
to nudge some memory
from its box under the bed
of that childhood you put to rest
twenty some years ago.

That box is also full of dust—
adobe from the ranch
in New Mexico. If you breathe
deep at the edge of this chord,
you smell the flint
of the summer thunderstorm
bullying its way over Chaco peak.
Here, at this run, the rain
on sandstone. And in this tone,

what is it? Something lost, the thing gone,
but not the feeling—
here's that rift, coyly
religious, it brings back the night
after seeing *The Ten Commandments*
in the back seat of the Dodge
you thought you could believe
in God, and so when you
sat late at your bedroom window,
looking east, toward the ruins
that some said was Villa's
hideout, a light grew
out of the tips of the junipers

like the burning bush,
you took it as a sign
and made promises to God
and soon forgot them,
until just now. And these
notes, this voice, make you
want to promise someone
something, anything, again.

But you've grown wise
to the ways of promise,
and hope rattles like wheels
on a gravel road you drive
looking for what you lost.
And sitting there on that bottom
step, the dust warming your toes
you know poetry
has music but isn't the song

that people listen to.
In his room your son
is singing. You've already
bought him a guitar.

Was that your father's gift,
the one promise he could keep,
alone with the page
and letters like notes
that struggled toward melody?

Poets' children learn
what their parents
refuse to believe:
that words are never enough
to make a grown girl sing.

RIDGE LINES

The trail pitched forward
then right and
left into a bowl
where firs grounded us
in scanty shade.
Below

the valley drifts
and glazes
in its own heat.

A nuthatch blurs the air
with his tuneless song.

Higher
grouse thump.
They elude our eyes;
we stare at the sound;
it holds us here
like a face from the past
we can't quite place.

We shift our packs
and three feet on,
coming or going
we can't quite tell:
a rubber boa
dull as adobe
sledges the dirt.

We circle at a distance,
slow like horses circle sheep
in the pastures below,
each move meant
to make our presence felt,
to make some sense of fear
at one so small and still.

All day caution shallows
our breathing like dust.

RED HILLS AND BONES

The March tulips bloom
cruel and lovely every year—
wanted/unwanted, needed/refused
you were the winter
child, too late to choose.

Through doubt, then tests,
and finally fever,
resist/persist.
It was spring and your brother
laughed loud in the greening sun
while you curled—a question
mark/marked.

When you let go, I rose
from sleep as branches lift
with the release of snow.
Your weight had no bearing
and gravity was gone.

By morning, blood like sunrise
lit the sheets.

Losing you was harder
than what truth I can
tell you now; that grief
was real, daughter.

Ten years it's taken
to deliver you here
on this page, to a house
too small for you.

Outside this window
clematis climbs the ladder
of summer, eager and blue,
beside it the sweet white
irony of baby's breath.
I planted both for you.
Now, I give you up
to memory, to the tulips'
empty stalks.

I will learn to love without its object
and to believe it is enough.

CIRCUMNAVIGATING LOSS

With seven children and a wife,
my father-in-law did not need me
to share his death.
He was one who knew the uses of a joke,
how it could clarify the chaos,
that ruffled kinship, the sound
he navigated full sail ahead,
like the wind of the valley
he was born and raised in.
Compliments were always oblique
and we who loved him learned
to read currents of connection
and measure the depths
of what could not be said.

The last time I saw him
adrift in the antiseptic fog
of a hospital bed, I knew
there was nothing I could say
that wouldn't sink like lead
dragging its lost leader
to the bottom, so I said
I love you and bent to kiss
his cheek and he, seeing me,
lifted his head.

It was awkward as it's always been,
nose to chin, bungling our final
troublesome kiss. That's how
I left him. Now I love the awkward
accuracy of that moment,
as one who loves to sail
must love the darkness that defines
the edges of a constellation we can't read.

SUNDAY AT ST. ANDREW'S

How baroque my Protestant
hands, lying still, folded,
useless in my lap as dead doves,
soft, smothered in the folds
of my dress.

How conspicuous their stillness
here among these other hands
that fly from lips to heart,
from forehead to chest
right then left,
then back again
effortlessly
as if these bodies were trees and
the priest's words an ornate wind
that moved them limb by limb
through gold-leafed light
under the glassy gaze of saints.

And how thick my Protestant lips
as I mouth God's word—
is she counting my mistakes
this woman kneeling next to me—
whose every word is right on cue,
around whose hand a rosary
is wrapped like brass knuckles.

Here, the history of holy conscription
rattles in the offering plate,
the pure ones on parade. Alone
in the pew, the smell of my guilt
grows stronger as they return
from the holy sip, orderly, penitent
forgiven and cleansed,
relief as palpable
as rain. And yet at service's

end we shake on it, walk out
into the clear cool day. But even
here, the ordinary has been sacrificed:
traffic lights blink like stained glass,
urge caution, command us stop and
suddenly I accelerate hoping to be caught
ticketed and retained: a chance to
plead guilty, to pay big
and drive home clean.

NOT EASY

these mornings of the gray streaked sky,
clouds breaking up, light breaking in.
Even the blackened branches against the day
do not move, but splay themselves needy
and itching for weather. This is the calligrapher
of doubt who scribes the white between the lines.

Not easy, this heart, these hands together again.
Some days, it's heart in hand; others, hand over heart.
Neither satisfies. Needy couple, they. One looking
for love, the other for work; both wanting it honest
and hard, not easy, not free, but clear. Not easy

this season between winter and spring. Literal
and dry, absent of irony. The bones on the mat
of lawn simply lie, white and bare. Even the dog
won't tend them in this off season, season without name,
season without ease or anger. Be still.

Dance the space between the steps; it is not stillness.
Hear the music between the notes; it is not silence.
Read the white between the lines; it's not empty.
Here to gather. Breathe, stare, blink. This stillness
is motion, this silence is music, the white space sings.

FLOWERS: MEMORIAL DAY

They are the beautiful dying gift
we bring our beautiful dead,
their numbers etched in marble,
molded in bronze under their names.
We read them now like books
on the shelf above our bed
whose titles bring back a scene
or two, more clearly than the face,
the voice, the way he flicked ashes
from a cigarette, the way she wiped
a plate or slurred a phrase.

Children run among the graves
finding this a fine place to play
their parents quiet
for once, like at the table
just before grace, leaving them

strangely to their noisy games.
Theirs is the sweet irony
of cut iris, stems sucking water
from coffee cans and plastic cups,
not yet knowing the absence of roots,
the numbered hours, the weightlessness
of a name in stone on a sunlit day.

TWO YEARS
Joan Bourne, 1946-2000

and the luxury of grieving is gone.
Time holds the fact of us
leaning into each other
as the sun dropped over Ios—
your arm on my shoulder
in the photo. The backdrop,
bougainvillea and white-washed arches,
fact into *artifact* into *artifice*,
a weary procession. You died.

I say it now, and notice these
willed transitions, as if the poem
were itself a death
to indulge and finally
divest oneself of. To end
on a preposition expecting more.
Sad transparences.

Now we are framed by irises,
transparent too. What light are we
that breaks as briefly as the flash
on film? As bright?

I've little left to lose
but years and your scent
held for a while in the scarf
you wore that night half blown
on ouzo and gossip, goat bells
ringing the old stars in.

What we wanted was beyond us—
now I love desire
for its own sweet distance.
I lift my glass—
another year starts tomorrow.

SOBER AND SANE

How similar by choice
the sober and the sane.

Each choosing
every hour not to wait
on their despair;

each feeling on the right
hand that their drug
is always near.

Chained to a corpse
they're muled in the rut,
circling the mill
of their own making,
stone on stone
and grinding.

Every day the grist
of self ground fine
and finer by repetition.

But the sober and the sane
by choice know the path
is deep and flat.

They know theirs
is a circling back
to cover the self-
same ground.

They know that every day
they pass the moment
of their choosing;
that in their passing,
corpse in tow,
drug in sight,

that mercy is a menace
and forgiveness found
in flight.

SPEAKING TO THE DEAD

It makes no difference, really,
in what tongue—for they
have forgotten how the lips
curl around an "o" or how the tongue
thrusts itself into conversation
without thought. Some will call you out
into the night, alone, to send
their message home: *Love,
I'm sorry; no room left
for anger. Be well. Move on.*

But who can listen to such
and not stand still under the pinprick
light of the stars, those stingy pores,
wanting more, always more.
Wishing to tie *being* to a rock, to anchor
this thought against darkness—
not death, but its certainty.

The man I've loved
for thirty years remembers
a sunrise over Menton
and a beautiful young woman
boarding the train he was on—
lovely and lucid, but silent
as tongues of fire. I want
to say, "Don't look
to the sun. At night the dead speak.
Listen. Step out."

For in the dark
our own train hollows the distance
from *here* to *there*—it is the difference
of one letter turned sound; it is the line
we will not cross, it is the track
carrying the train on and on
under the streaming tongue
of its own exhaust, sound
outrunning the silence
it must become.

SWEETER STILL

MORNING SONGS

These are the old songs
I sing them a capella.

I sing these small songs
in front of a dark window
before morning comes.

I sing these cold songs
knowing no one will hear
the notes shiver.

DECONSTRUCTING HEART

Take the *r* out of *heart*,
feel the *heat*. Kiss the flame.
Step into the fire. Get burned.
Temper desire.

Take the *he* out of *heart*,
make *art*. Easier to see
than love; harder to make.

Take the *her* out of *heart*,
there's where you're *at*.
At the mercy of the moment,
fully present, attending—
at the end, at first glance.

Take the *ear* out of *heart*
and you won't hear
the consonance of *h & t*
when they meet without
vowels to interfere:
the sound the finger
and thumb make
around the candle's flame
to snuff it out.

Take the *eat* out of *heart*,
you'll starve in the whir
of the *h* & the *r* as they huddle
over their empty plate
and can't tell you
where it hurts.

Hear her art, her try,
her start, to reconstruct
this too parsed
heart.

GRAVITY: SEMANTICS

Gliding glance
of wing on air,
this swift now slits
the blueless sky—
cares nothing
for my wish to sing,
to burden move
with meaning,
to feather out the day
with colors
too bright for cheer,
to make flight
more than fancy—
a strict necessity
of form—and not
this clever beauty
waiting, heavy
on my tongue.

LOGIC

Last night
a wind rattled the house

and a sycamore by the ditch
went down. Now a wren

hops from branch
to branch and back

in odd dimension
with her world

or hangs headlong
to quiz the ground.

I know that vertigo too,
how some days we wake

and our lives have been reordered
by accident, leveled by the logic

of trees falling a breath beyond us,
as we sleep.

DRIFT

Drift tonight.
Let nothing hold you
to this room with one light
burning like a lily on its stalk.
If something darker
than this eleven o'clock
window calls you out,
be led. It's only
a small voice
needing breath.
Yours.

PERIODIC TABLEAU

This, an elegant experiment
where scientific discourse meets a rhyme
and molecule and syllable invent
the scheme the schemer thought she had in mind.

But formula includes itself the form,
as heart embodies heat and art and hate,
as momentum to its moment must conform
and logos to its logic relegates

some logarithmic sign predicting sense
in outcomes we can't forecast or conceive.
And yet our failures offer recompense
for intuition's errors and logic's greed:

an antidote to apomictic bliss—
for what is elemental will persist.

YOU AND I

In *ingenious* that bright *i*
following its *n* like flame follows
the candle down the wick

is me subjective, moodily introspective,
the flame as it sparks and sputters,
stares and stutters into
the melt of its own making.

But this is not the way of candles.
Cast for romance and religion,
small celebrations, they remind us
we, too, are crawling down the cord
of our own burning. So,

that bright I, second person, is you,
the tough *u* in *ingenuous*,
who, like Lauren Bacall
appears just when the story gets slow,
drags you in to strike a match,
smoke trained to follow an old flame

and the possibility of an ingenious I
is snuffed by that ingenuous you
as fire, all longing burned away,
finds us, locking arms at last,
united in sweet ennui.

LIMITS

Remember the Japanese restaurant
we entered that night
out of the dreary weather? And the child
waiter in a black velvet bow tie
who sat down in the next room
and watched as we ate chicken
and prawns? How the hour
pushed in around us as if
there was nothing better to do?

Later the cook came out too,
wiping his hands on a dirty apron
and looked out the window,
deep into his own reflection.

When the child brought us dessert,
an apple cut and assembled
to resemble a swan,
it was difficult not to admire
too loudly, not to wonder
at the contradictions
that brought us all here.

In that fog, only the outlines
were visible, every street
closed down around itself,
a ten o'clock curfew. But
we saw the limits of hope
in the too generous tip we left,
coins like dull eyes on a dark
table the night had set.

WHAT WAITS TO BE SAID?

Just outside this window in dark, in heavy snow,
the owl has come back
to her favored perch in the cottonwood.
Her notes shut down the night
limb by limb.

And in the time between
her last syllable and the first light
you might hear what waits to be said.

Turn your head to the side
and stop your breath: A word
will drop on your tongue like lime.

Breathe again, give it voice.
Let it be bitter and fragrant as thyme,
resonant as snow on snow.

This stillness
between morning and night
wants only silence. Go slow:

send out a sound, like the owl.
Give it a body of fur,
the squawk of a jay,
teeth of the rat.

Your words, your voice.
Don't take them back.

GREEN VALLEY, MARCH

Even at night the Arizona sky is big,
crickets already sing-saw from the edge
of the wash. The green stays grey
as it will during the day, but the poppies,
the poppies have waited out two years
of drought—for this, this year, the best
in twenty-five to powder the draws.
They are the color of caution, blinking
and bright. The surprise of saffron,
changeable in wind. The color of luck—
the first hot day and we are in it,
humbled at the edge of plenitude,
brighter than any city full-lit on a clear night,
inhabited by no one, indifferent
as we were last night sitting at the city's edge.

BERRY PICKING

A nagging summer wind
pushed us after berries,
blackcaps nodding
drunk in their own juice.

Birds fretted the creek-side brush
and we lost ourselves awhile
in their noises, in the work of hands,
in the rhythm of berries falling,
slowly filling buckets with their purple plop.

Our eyes learned a new obsession,
fingers risked themselves, unthinking,
for the plumpest: a pinch of thigh,
a pout, a kiss. Even the snakes
that startled the grass at our feet
couldn't disturb that hour of work,

that gift from no one we simply took
in the guiltless greed of plenty.

THE DAY IS SUDDENLY LONGER

After wine, then brandy,
dim music and wondering aloud
after friends whose lives
seemed clearer than our own,
we came at last to poetry
and all its disclaimers.

Stepping outside,
audience to snow's light,
star's light, we felt the judgment
of that late winter night.

After making love, then small
talk, we slept, dreamless
willing accomplices to nothing
more than our own breathing
and woke late
into another day.

The sun had risen
and beveled light
in dusty corners,
lit a current of color
through the faded carpet
roses, over the unmade bed.

After muffins, jam,
and morning speech
awakening
we enter that room again
for a brush or book and,
hand outstretched, stopped
startled, to feel
the absolute change
that angle of light had made.

HORSES

are about heat:
in the curve that aligns
shoulder and neck
where the sweat begins;
at the ticklish flank
where the hair whorls
and the skin thins;
at the velvet juncture
of girth and foreleg;
in the crease behind
the back-turned ear;
in the sweet big breath
that wants yours
and smells your cheek.

And they are about earth:
mud packed into perfect V's
of the frog; three-quarter moon
prints down the familiar track
to the willow tree where in summer
they find shade, each other,
and head to tail flick and shudder
the flies away; the flat dusting
place where they clunk down
to roll, clumsy leggy bodies like beetles aback,
then up again on all fours
they shake the dust about themselves,
the storm from which they'll emerge
absolved of all disgrace.

They are about wind:
in which they stand tail to
and head down enduring & durable
because they know how to move
the air; because they know
how the wind shapes itself
around them, and their bodies
are the shape that shelter takes.

EPIPHANIES AT FORTY-EIGHT

Most mornings it hurts
to get out of bed: back, knee,
head. Rise slowly, sun.

Face in the mirror,
you are mine behind those lines.
I rub the glass clean.

Breasts, gravity calls.
Turn your noses up, girls. Bag
that old boy's whistle.

In the coffee shop
the man eyeing my bare arms
thinks of his sister.

I watch my mother.
How will I age? Suddenly
sixty seems young.

I've learned to like scotch
on the rocks again. Good scotch
with generous friends.

What the head forgets
the heart remembers, mostly—
doesn't miss a beat.

I am more patient
with our old black lab who snores
through our lovemaking.

At forty-eight, I
began counting syllables
at night, alone, content.

Fingers thrum the desk
navigating distances,
no compass, no star.

CROWS

Sun transcribes
berry vines
as morning wakes

beyond this window
some small measure
of hope finds
one crow

a piece of bread,
carries it
to the warming road.

Another, close by,
hops over.

Another,
flies down.

Two more drop
from branches
like dead weight.

There is no struggle here,
but the gawk and squawk,

the casual insistence
of those
who must scrounge
a living

counting less
on the crumbs of kindness
than the thoughtless
casting away.

BREAD AND WINE

The farmer knows
the seed of bread is hard,
the labor of grapes bitter.

And his wife knows his hands
ache some nights. In his sleep
they pull blue beetles from clusters.

Should she wake him from his work,
knowing from her own that bread
has leniency and leverage,

wine resolution of character.
He would only want to check
the weather, and unable to sleep

find his way to her kitchen,
recall her hands working the dough,
pour a small glass of red

and in it, soften a crust,
believe again
in the leniency of memory.

THIS NIGHT

How sweet to be awake
past midnight in July,
under a full moon,
a few stars salting
the sky. To see the line
of hills and feel the pasture
rise around the bedded
bodies of the horses,
to hear the coyote clamor
just far enough beyond
the edge of the pond
where the kildeer
scuttles her nest
against the frenzied
song. Sweeter still

to open the door
and enter the house
full of sleeping sounds,
the old dog snoring
in the kitchen, the last
of the day's laundry
tumbling round and round,
the hollow flutter of a moth,
between the shade and bulb.

The jars of jelly, blackcap
now, purpling the counter,
left out to be admired,
a small job done. The dishes
drying in the sink. The hall
light on and in the study
a window open to the smell
of sage and lavender in bloom.

How sweet to feel
the need to say,
to no one listening
anywhere that *this*
is all and well and good.

BRANDING TIME

One by one the calves
go down to dust, stretched
by ropes between two horses,
pulled by the ligament of fear
toward a human smell.

Is it the angled limb
that brings to mind the martyrs
at Meteora, ankles & elbows bound,
stretched between heaven and earth,
heads wrenched sideways
as if in ecstasy? Did they smell
God in all this blood?

How lovingly
their torments are preserved,
their dying moments burned
in muted colors across the chapel walls
as if to prove ownership prevails
and is all.

The calf's throaty bawl,
the thick incense of branding time,
bring me back to iron and hair,
to the delicate flame, smoke and flesh
melting in air. Lazy 7K, left hip
and he's one of ours: branded,
dehorned, vaccinated, castrated.
We watch him struggle, stagger,
jump away to join the others
huddled at the gate, shriven sinners.

I can't pretend I didn't like those days—
the men spitting & swearing, the horses sweating,
heat and leather, spurs and sage.

How strange the memory
that heels, then drags you through dirt.
Were those bells I heard in Greece
or the ringing of rowels across
the monastery floor?

And, don't we all martyr ourselves
to a time and place not of our making?

In truth, those saints seemed quaint,
their deaths a parody of *Divine*.
Maybe Christ is just a good ole boy
sitting on the fence, counting heads,
marking time, one of a dying breed
like the rest of us, hoping for an early
spring, a herd worth hauling to the sales ring,
and the sweet incense of burning flesh—
nothing more than the past, like us, he won't let die.

WINTER FRUIT
—For Joe

When the snow came,
heavy and early, some trees
still clung to fruit, apples mostly,
undesirable in their wrinkled
bird pocked skins, worm scarred.

But the snow covered them
like a lover's hand cupped lightly
over the curve of another's. And so
made them beautiful again.

In the sun they were planets
in a chartable universe,
shedding light and reflective.
At night, they swam the dark
currents, and sometimes
would bulge the skin of moonlight
like a trout heaving water against air.

The fruit grew heavier in their frozen
form and all around them the branches
bent, broke free, or hung by threads of bark—
the tree made awkward by their tenacity.
But apples held as if this
cold beauty was it and all.

Who's to know?
Who's to know what beauty,
grace, or favor can be granted
by the weight of early snow.

After three days, the weather broke.
Limbs sprung free and dropped
their leaves, penitent now, after
all their foolish longing. But the apples,
the apples, they refused to release.
And though it snowed again,
nothing made them what
they once had been.

Later, when the season
left little choice, the birds found
them hanging in their brown skins
and took up where they'd left
off in fall. Perhaps they found
them sweeter, too, tempered by ice.

OLIVE LIGHT

IN OLIVE LIGHT

Zakynthos
Light oils the leaves of olive trees,
falls in slats across the white road.
At my back the sound of bells—
a distant church, and closer,
goats orchestrate a hillside.
Ahead, a motorcycle churns
the morning heat. Foreign
but familiar, the blooms
along the cut-bank—wild rose,
chicory, pink morning glory
the bees cannot abandon.

A wedge of rock, smoothed now,
shapes a broken satyr's hoof.
The bone-white roots calcify
but thrive. Ageing, ageless Aegean.

Athens
The sad zoo at the center
of the National Gardens
houses chickens, pea fowl,
a tattered cockatoo, a single sulking vulture.
The people who find their way here,
leave dull-eyed,
drawn to nearby Hadrian's gate
or the temple of Zeus where
Heracles slays a lion
in magnificent relief.

In the relentless Athenian sun
they wonder at the hand
that cared to carve the curl
in a beard, the muscle bunched
for the impact it will never feel,
a tooth sunk deep in marble flesh
while somewhere in the Plaka,
disguised in rags,
a god shakes a coin in a tin cup.

STILL LIFE: ZAKYNTHOS

Two eggs,
one pear.
A brown leaf
on a stem.
A square
metal plate

and the sun-burned
backdrop of
green bamboo.

Vines shining.
Eggs the milky brown
of Zante soil,
goat's milk
and almond nougat.

Who could not want
this life,
still?

*

Three chickens wobble,
walk without a clue
about our need for order.

The military planes
fly formation:
a perfect triangle
against Aegean blue.

Four pigeons
white as plaster
in the sun,
rise, twist, dive
into a cypress row,
whose spires
needle these contradictions
of space and place and time.

A CALLING

The bells peal on the half hour,
calling the faithful back and back:
the old men in wool suits,
the old women in black.

They fill the streets
where their grandchildren
spent the night smoking and singing,
where the cats they will not own
or abandon piss and scratch
and eat food set out beneath windows
curtained with lace overlooking
dumpsters bristling with shoes,
sweaters, shopping baskets
the conspicuous trash
of a new middle class.

In this city,
tourists wander their streets,
admire their trash, stop to photograph
the men in suits and women in black,
their cats, the life they did not choose,
and all its glorified refuse. But
these faithful have grown weary
of the glare, the sheen of history
reflected in the marble curbs,
the invasion by yet another culture,
its constant demands. And so they
speak only to each other under
the wagging tongues of bells.

ATHENS & ANASAZI

Canaries lilt the morning alive.
The concrete truck arrives
to pump its load—the building
down the street is going up
another level. Men shout;
horns bark then howl;
and always cabs and motorbikes
rattle and roar through these
steel and stone ravines.

The canyons of my childhood
were made of stone. Under
their cliffs, Anasazi ground maize
listening to water drip
through sandstone
and piñon jays quarrel
the heat into evening.
The stone church
lost deep in the canyon
stood for years,
abandoned and unharmed.

But here the rubbled single
story across the street,
mud bricks and rock
that in my country
would be named
history and monumented,
will soon be gone.
A remnant of life without heights,
of a poorer past better let gone.

When the Old Ones left
most think it was for lack
of water, lack of corn. They
made their way up the canyon
walls, and were gone. Their
country was mine, their history
was not. This history is mine,
this country is not.

Its light is the light of lemons
glowing in blue shade. I'll take
that small piece with me
to hold, to hold without hands,
as it disappears into history.

IN KIFFISIA

the women wear
Dior and Channel.
They glide from shop
to shop on marble walks
and sip café frappes
in the red shade
of bougainvillea
reassured, charmed
by the music
of their phones
and car alarms.

Their indifference to
sculpted breads on baker's shelves;
the naked butchered bird,
feet intact, a fisted proof;
evening gossip in the plateia;
quince paste, pomegranate red
and heavy in its cellophane,
cool as the marble disks
we carried back from Ios—
wanting to stroke the curve
of a stone arm, to feel its weight.

I am a tourist needing a past
they need to move beyond:
I find their common exotic;
they eye my durable shoes,
my stout American legs.

MELTEMI

In Athens, the women wear black.
The old ones sack themselves
in woolen skirts and shawls &
headscarves, scuffle the streets
of their past in black flats.

The young prefer leather
jackets and minis,
hair loose and black
or French red, Danish blonde,
but always haute. Paris
is their city, everything
they want. Between these,

the middle-aged. Their daughters
are what they wanted to be;
their mothers what they become.
And so they wear soft colors:
the greens of olive leaves
and capers whose fruit
and flowers are not metaphor
but a delicate moment on the tongue:
a sharp yet sweet delight,
memory that has bloomed.
Or the yellow of cornmeal,
lentils, crème caramel;
and that bleu of newborn eyes.
I know those colors well.
As I know

color is a sentence we've strung
between two poles: then, the past,
and then, tomorrow. Color denies
darkness, defiles it without need
to reconcile ourselves to that other
desperation. We'll wear them now,
hung between these two,
like laundry on a line,
shivering in the warm Athenian wind.

THE GREEK SUN

The sun on grape leaves strikes
a chord, *A* minor. The sun
on olives, tremolos, *B*-flat.
The sun on bamboo wavers,
arpeggios. The sun on tile
roofs blunts a middle *C*.

The sun on lavender exacts iambic.
Sun on fading poppies: trochee.
The dactyl lisps on hibiscus tongues.
Bougainvillea makes metaphor,
blue sky, a cliché.
In this, land of ouzo and honey, music & poetry,
and the hot blue sea on a cloudless day.

HOMESICK

The light here is bright,
the Aegean sea
warming into summer.

It's been cold at home,
morels not yet up.
Here the strawberries
are at an end, cherries coming on.

No, it's not news were hungry for
but home itself: a house, animals,
land. And old appetite returns
as after an illness. The sweet sip
of morning in the garden
by the pond, the musty spice

of the closet where I've stuffed
leather bags and shoes, cedared
woolens against moths; the salt
of the chicken coop; the sweet
herb of the sorrel mare's breath—
how suddenly and subtly the bitter
sweet and green of foreign fruits
can bring a traveler home.

ARRIVAL

O'Keefe's poppies bloom
on a postage stamp.
In my garden a red anemone
sparks memory:
Hania and bells.

I've left; I'm home.
Lavender and sage,
bunch daises, push
through crab grass.

Balsam blooms
and the wind blows,
cottonwoods drape
Greek cypresses
in down: white columns

on Aegina. Apollo
mediates the distance
between there and then,
here and now.

WILD STRAWBERRIES: REECER CREEK

At last a myth resolves:
Homer ignites Achilles'
red-gold hair

the shade of wild berries
I found covered
in roadside dust.

The years I've waited
for this chance harvest
now arrive and sit
with me, cross-legged
for the Spartan feast.

The bells of Crete
are ringing in the heat
of summer. Wild
goats graze on thyme.

Did I travel and return
just for this?
Strawberries
sweeter than slow-dripping
honey. The fruits
of a dry land,
ripen cleverly.

AGAINST SILENCE

LI CH'ING-CHAO IN THE CCU

        Tired of the curtain,
its blue lotus promising health,
I rise and wrap my thin gown
around my thighs, hold it closed
at the back. In the next room

an ancient woman in a wheelchair
describes her pain. The man
one curtain over listens to Leno.
The TV shines like a moon
on his face. I am alone
with my heart, beating, beating.

        The IV curls from my hand,
wayward root of the plum tree,
and the nurse with fingers of spring
taps it, for blood, for truth and proof
life will move on. Her eyes will not
meet mine. This is the business
of bad news.

        The old woman moans
and Leno's audience laughs. Outside,
the ice thickens and the distant dog barks.
The sound rolls down the lotus tongues,
catches in their throats.

CHIMAYO

Crutches hang in rows,
wheelchairs stacked five high—
I count them as I roll by
walker wheels dusted red
with Chimayo dirt the color
of dried blood on gauze.
We come here
on crutches,
canes
wheels
on braced legs
on a wing
and a prayer,
paraplegic fliers
needing the miracle of updraft
on a windless day.
We light candles,
kneel,
pray to the powers
that be
for our very being.
In the sanctuary back room
someone has dug a hole
and filled it with imported sand—
the original dirt long gone—
to be applied like salve
on knees, heads, arms,
to be eaten.
We ingest hope
to reflect the terroir
like a good wine.
But in this landscape of miracles
terror is but an "i" away—
eye for eye,
tooth for bloody tooth.
Unhealed, unclean
we slouch toward
the sanctuary store,
beasts burdened
with small bags of dirt
blaming our failure to heal
on our too fickle faith.
We buy a candle and chili,

a t-shirt advertising the Day of the Dead
in bare-boned humor,
a wooden saint,
tangibles to lay hands on.
We leave unchanged:
simple tourists who came looking
for a map or miracle to lead us
beyond our own inglorious end.

WALKING ON STILTS

My son must learn
to walk on stilts,
to morph his six feet
into nine,
to become the imposing
ghost of Christmas Present,
cloaked in flowing robes,
red bearded and brazen.
On stage,
each step is carefully crafted and marked
as he learns
the body's tipping point,
its fulcrum, its old fear of falling.
I, too, am learning
this trick of consciousness.
Every day I wake
and test my legs,
having lowered my expectations,
heightened my sense of gravity.
This disease of diminishing,
without returns,
means each day I must
take stock of the body,
determine what is going today,
recall what is already gone.
My doctor says, "You will know!"
meaning I will know
the beginning
of each new end.
Disintegration
will follow its own
winding path—
tongue to lips,
lips to cheek,
an ironic Easter twitch
of the nose.
And so every step becomes
both miracle,
and manacle.
Teaching my son to walk,
we measured
the steps to insure success
and with arms outstretched

caught him as he fell.
That was our reward
for the distance he covered.
His falling was a joy,
and learning to walk
was means to a happy end.
My stuttering steps
reveal the prodigal child
come home to drool and cry,
to hiccup and fall,
and always
at inopportune times.
But now, still
as much mother as child,
I want to be there
fully when I fall,
I want to learn the trick of
falling. Graceful and even grateful,
I want to make my peace with this grave
and unjust ground.

I AM THINKING OF MY GRANDMOTHER'S HOUSE ON STEELE STREET

its scent of face powder
and brick, of green potatoes
in the basement sink. So when
my son stops mid-lift,
halfway between chair and bed,
and burrows his nose in my hair,
I dangle limp, obedient in his thick hands.
My head lists left against his shoulder
and he inhales— a slow deep breath
meant to remember.
What hangs in the balance there
between breaths, between now and then,
the end we both feel coming?
The moment morphs into a presence
almost palpable.
I am a burden he must bear
despite my best intentions.
We hold our breath…

Isn't it always a question of holding on
or letting go? Of gauging the waters' pull
against our need to anchor fast?

My son exhales.
He swings me into bed
straightens my legs
pulls the sheet to my chin.
We are casting off
waiting for the boat to free itself
of rocks and ballast
to slip weightless
into this unfamiliar current.
A little tug and we're free.
I'm adrift;
he waves, holding steady on shore:
memory silvers the surface
then dives deep.

One day may he,
in some sweet exhalation of willow,
remember not this weight,
but the smell of rosemary
and linen caught in my hair.

AGAINST SILENCE

> *Silence is more eloquent than words.*
> *Speech is of time, silence is of eternity.*
> —Thomas Carlyle

Before the eloquence of silence
comes the tongue's bumbling slur.
I learn quickly to avoid the ells.

Por favor (in English) becomes peas.
(And in this disease,
the transition to vegetable matter
is slow but certain, as sure as the seed
becomes vine and bears fruit
that splits into seed. And so on.)

Shortly after the ells, the tees depart,
bees no longer buzz, cees cease.
The inconstant consonants recede.
But the inviolate vowels bloom
and I ahh, ew and ohh
my way through the day
as if newly blessed by what
I see, surprised at what I say.

Never mind that the voice I hear
before I speak is the same voice
I've known for years. Never mind
that the woman at the coffee shop
asks for my order twice. Never mind
that the man at the table nearby glances
up wondering if I am drunk or merely
stupid, then looks away ashamed.
His shame is of the moment
and for a moment we share it silently.

But silence is of eternity and this world
is meant for speech. So, bumble tongue
and lips lisp your way through ineloquent
nonsense; desire babble your syllables—
until you are the spectacle of sound,
until the vowels close around you
like a shroud, muffled and worn
but warm, warm as the first word
your mother's face above you uttered.

THE RED-WINGED BLACKBIRDS ARE BACK

you say, but your voice is flat and grey
as the ice on the pond and suddenly that scene out the window—
the white bark of the birch, the black bird,
the mat of pond ice—is flat too, shallow as a photo
we've stepped unwillingly into.
For twenty-two springs we've stood at this window
and watched those birds return to patrol the feeders,
winter relieved by their throaty trills, the promise of tulips
and berries carried on their wings.

Now, love, there is no promise. Still, we are here.
Watching and listening as spring moves in. Just yesterday
two mourning doves bobbed in parody around the tree—
let's leave that one be. We have come this far. It must do.
It must be enough now to thrill, even in sadness,
to the blackbird's song.

Let's step across this dark window's sill,
the one you gave me long ago in a poem. Listen.
I will be back next spring—noisy, bossy, brassy.
Look for me. I will be the one dressed in black
still wearing my heart, yours, on my sleeve.

poem of one thumb

has no punctuation
no capitals
to slow its stiff work
left&right&up&down
indifferent to rules
the work of a hammer
seeking the nail's head
the work of a hand
genuflecting
as if to bless the page
with its clumsy lumbering
as if grace might reside
among these words taking
slow shape
despite the tremulous antics
of one sad digit
in search of a true line
one level without the slur of irony
without rancor or need

if that shyster in the green visor offered me a deal
trade this body
for the knowledge gained
in its diminishing
would I take the bait
or play the hand I have

this opposable right thumb
lonely as it is
refuses to fold
and in one smooth arc
from left to right & up
finds the way
from *n* to *o*
and so I play on

SILENCE

We fill our solitude with sound,
warm and bitter,
the way we fill our cups with
tea or coffee,
hoping they will fill us
in turn.
Even the glass that's drained
can sing:
run a finger around the rim &
hear the bells
of emptiness
ring.

TOWARD EARTH

Just beyond the ragged scruff of willows
that edge our pasture, my son is flying
his red kite. His is serious play. The kite,
a mode of transport as much as music or booze
to some, a door into that private room
where we face only ourselves in judgment,
no mirrors or windows to trap our reflection,
to interrupt our longing, sometimes, for longing
itself. Now a red wing dips toward earth and
drags like a kildeer its invitation to defend
against the clawed cat's lonely amusements,
against the mind's measure of tomorrow.

Now the red kite arcs upward and shudders
at the moment of greatest torque,
at the live weight of my son holding it there,
for me I'm sure, sharing his delight,
two listening for the audible sigh of the red kite
against the scriptless sky.

Is it my mother loneliness for words that holds
my breath, that draws me again and again
to the window but keeps me at the pasture gate?
I stalk my own silence here,
carried into this lost hour on a red kite.

LAST BOAT RIDE
Priest Lake, August 2011

Of course I thought of Charon as hands lifted
my dead weight into my son's arms. He might have been a boatman
in a different time or place, his biceps
the size of young pines harvested here,
perfect for a litter or wikiup, perfect for bearing the dead
to sacred ground or pyres. But he's no undertaker, this son of mine,
who vibrates with the stories under his skin
so eager to be loosed they fracture his every silence, splay
and animate his arms in fits of telling. What animus drives him so deep
inside himself not even the Mother tongue can rouse him? So even now,
in the gravity of this transport, I feel in him a fire kindling in his chest and
suddenly he breaks into song: *Yo heave ho! Yo heave ho! It's into the boat we
go!* And we are back again, dogs milling underfoot, the dock and boat rising
and falling under Joe's anxious instructions, our laughter, old friends in an
old ritual—the last boat ride—under the pulse of a full moon, the blind rush
of the Pleiades falling all around us, invisible campfires on Kalispell Island,
smoke rising through pine boughs. No more than this moment in a shared
life, the briefest bloom of a lavender poppy whose seed contains all our summers here, even this one still unraveling.

Into the perfect evening light, we set off, six seeking closure, one life
at a time. This time it's mine.

Wedged between husband and friend, head lolling with the music
(intentionally upbeat), I try to gather all the nights into this one coming
on too fast. Port side the full moon rising; starboard, the sun setting. The
perfect metaphor spins us into ribbons of light across the water. We must
not say what we are thinking, we must not think what we are thinking: the
moment is that fragile. If I could speak, I would break into song so loud the
trees would shudder and nod, waking to one note of joy shattering the lake
like glass. On shore my son waits, spinning his own tale of love's struggle to
be made fast and sound.

A POEM CONSIDERING LOVE

> *it isn't possible to love what*
> *one refuses to know.*
> —Louise Gluck

Loving is a way to leave.

What moves the grass
when we are still?

I am standing,
waiting to be moved.
Look at me.

I want to touch your hand
and not know it.

I want to lie down
in the grass and hear it
move around me.

I want your hands
to move over me,
wind over grass.

But beneath the field
a door is opening.

Leaving, too, is a way to love.

Touch my hand.
Know it.

THIS BODY OF DESIRE

> *"The degree to which we desire the physical*
> *is the degree to which we are separate from God."*

Between me and God,
this body,
designed for desire:

A Frans Gold Bar,
a Tangeray 10 martini,
dry, with three olives
at five-fifteen,
while Judy Collins sings
"Amazing Grace."

Between me and God
the dun mare's soft muzzle
on my neck,
the smell of wet cement,
or lavender, and dust.

Between us
my husband's full lips on mine,
like they used to be,
his hand on my nipple, my thigh,
a supple tongue in my mouth,
his, or mine.
I desire both.

And between me and God
a warm slice of bread
dipped in garlic spiked with oil.

My feet in turtle-backed water
on Psilli Amos Beach;
the smoke of incense rising
in the cave of the Apocalypse
and my hand in the pocket of stone
where Saint John placed his.
The granite now worn smooth
as marble by 2000 years of hands
wanting only to touch the stone

that touched the hand
the hand that touched God,
in the flesh.

Physical, and so full of desire.
We are flesh burning
for flesh, for food, for song,
for God.

Like the honeyed tapers
melting in the heat
of their delight at the touch
of flame to wick,
or the sweet smoke
rising up
out of this cold,
hard darkness

between God
and this
body of desire.

THE LAST WORD

Imagine this:
You are given
fifty words to speak,
no more.

Which would you choose?

Hello, I love you, thanks, goodbye
too easily said with hands and eyes.

No, first the names:
Joseph, Evan, Sarn, Selena.
Lois-Mother & Jacob-Father.
(You hyphenate here to
make them one and the ampersand
doesn't count.) Then,
(clever girl) no spaces between:
KarenKathyLailaLisaMarn:
that one would roll
off your tongue
like the muezzin calling
the faithful to prayer
in Khan-el-khalili, Cairo.
Naxos, Patmos, Delos
Sappello Corrales.

Next, *forgive me*.
This you would say
at least ten times.
Three syllables
to undo the errors
of a lifetime.

Then that line
heard in Mrs. Butterfield's
sixth grade class
(add her to the list)
that set words singing

*I must go down
to the sea again,
to the lonely sea
and the sand*

They never stopped.

But, when my tongue
lies flat in its fleshy cell,
will I still hear the words
as they used to sound?

Will their memory fade
like the scent
from a dead friend's scarf?

Perhaps I loved this voice
too much and the way I'd found
to sing without carrying a note.

But I will beg no pardon.
Let that pride precede my fall.

Let these sleek syllables
usher in the final lines
and run the tongue ragged
with their demands.

Listen for the last
word, the word that lasts:
listen.

Afterword: On Writing

I don't remember ever deciding to "be a writer." It didn't seem like it was something that was necessary to decide to be. Perhaps this was because I already knew it was the means that was given me to express, much as musicians know they will make music, or cooks know they will make feasts, or sculptors shape space. I don't mean to say that I have ever believed I was "gifted" in any sense; rather, I was born with a love for the feel and texture, the shape and music of language. Nothing more, nothing less.

I do know that I wrote early. Recently my mother returned a note to me that I had given her when I was 5 or 6. It said simply:

>   Mom,
> Looking for you on the world
>   To give you this
>   Love Judy

I don't know what the "this" was then . . . a few wildflowers or a drawing of a horse, perhaps. But now, these few words, for me, become the gift, that odd choice of preposition, *on*. My mother is a woman who is not in or of the world. She has never traveled around the world. She is one of those who moves behind the scenes, who makes things work in small ways, who is selfless and generous and so, is ON the world. I don't know why she saved the note; I'm not sure she knows. Perhaps parents intuit when it is their children have found the way given them to make it in the world. And that has been the primary function of writing in my life: it helps me make it through the world, it helps make sense of odd dimensions I find myself in.

Early on I wrote stories, not poems. I was fatally attracted to the drama of the horse as hero. My first stories were about horses who knew better than people how to survive and so they saved their riders from death by train or death by a stalking mountain lion. Later the stories transferred the heroics to people: the woman who leaped from the window of the hotel overlooking the Berlin Wall and was flung to freedom by the barbed wire! Then I discovered poetry.

I am pretty clear about the moment that the musical potential of language articulated itself to me. I was sitting in Mrs. Butterfield's 6th grade English class at Douglas Junior High School, row 3 seat 4, right behind Sylvia Padilla whose long black hair covered the back of her chair. We were just beginning the section on Poetry. Mrs. Butterfield opened her book, cleared her throat, and read:

> I must go down to the sea again, to the lonely sea and the sky
>   And all I ask is a tall ship and a star to steer her by.
> And the wheel's kick and the wind's song and the white sail's shaking,
>   And a gray mist on the sea's face, and a gray dawn breaking.

In that moment I think I understood that all the drama that I loved in my horse and human heroes could be contained in the more subtle power of a poem. Perhaps my family's move from the California coast to a rocky ranch in Las Vegas, New Mexico, had a lot to do with the response to Masefield's lines about the sea, but I think the moment of realization was inevitable. Somewhere, somehow, longing and language would discover me as they did that day, and the poems would begin.

It is fitting, I think, that another early poem I wrote included both my mother and Napoleon's horse. But ultimately it is also a poem about the power of language—to reveal and to heal. I think I have written most fervently when I was changing or suffering change. Poetry has provided a means to feel my way through moments that were fractured by grief or confusion. And because I am essentially shy and my mind shuts down during confrontation, poetry lets me cover territory after the fact. I am, I suppose, a post hoc poet, and like Theodore Roethke, a poet I admire, I too "think by feeling, what is there to know?"

—Judith Kleck

www.ingramcontent.com/pod-product-compliance
Lightning Source LLC
Chambersburg PA
CBHW031435150426
43191CB00006B/532